Aspects of P.E.

How Sport is Organized

Kirk Bizley

Heinemann
LIBRARY

www.heinemann.co.uk/library

Visit our website to find out more information about Heinemann Library books.

To order:

 Phone ++44 (0) 1865 888112

 Send a fax to ++44 (0) 1865 314091

 Visit the Heinemann Bookshop at www.heinemann.co.uk/library to browse our catalogue and order online.

First published in Great Britain by Heinemann Library, Halley Court, Jordan Hill, Oxford OX2 8EJ, part of Harcourt Education. Heinemann is a registered trademark of Harcourt Education Ltd.

© Harcourt Education Ltd 1999, 2007
The moral right of the proprietor has been asserted.

New edition first published in paperback 2008

Editorial: Andrew Farrow
Design: Joanna Hinton-Malivoire
Picture research: Hannah Taylor
Production: Alison Parsons

Originated by DOT Gradations Ltd
Printed and bound in China by CTPS

ISBN 978-0-431-07878-6 (hardback)
11 10 09 08 07
10 9 8 7 6 5 4 3 2 1

ISBN 978-0-431-07885-4 (paperback)
12 11 10 09 08
10 9 8 7 6 5 4 3 2 1

British Library Cataloguing in Publication Data
Bizley, Kirk
How Sport Is Organized. - 2nd ed. - (Aspects of P.E.)
1. Sports administration
I. Title
796'.069
A full catalogue record for this book is available from the British Library.

Acknowledgements

The publishers would like to thank the following for permission to reproduce photographs:

Action Plus/Glynn Kirk p21; Allsport pp11, 37; Allsport/Al Bello p43; Allsport/Bob Martin p18; Allsport/Pascal Rondeau p26; Colorsport p41; Dee Conway p31; Corbis/For Picture/Stephanie Reix p15; Corbis/Reuters/Gary Hershorn p42; Empics/AP p22; Getty Images p44; Getty Images/AFP/Adrian Dennis p32; Image Bank/Becker p19; J Allan Cash Ltd pp4, 30; Kos Picture Source/Peter Danby p27; Meg Sullivan pp5, 8, 9, 14, 20; Mike Brett Photography pp6, 24; National Coaching Federation pp25, 29; Oxford Brookes University Sport p28; Rex Features p7; Sporting Pictures (UK) Ltd p40; The Hulton-Deutsch Collection p38; The Hutchison Library p34.

Cover photograph of athletes at start reproduced with permission of Getty Images/Stone.

The author and publisher would like to thank Nuala Mullan and Doug Neate for their comments in the preparation of the first edition of this book. Our thanks to Oxford Brookes University Sport and Oxford City Rugby Club for their assistance during photo shoots.

Every effort has been made to contact copyright holders of any material reproduced in this book. Any omissions will be rectified in subsequent printings if notice is given to the publishers.

Contents

Any words appearing in the text in bold, **like this**, are explained in the Glossary.

How clubs are organized

Sport is organized at many different levels to match the standard at which any player may be taking part. Many famous sportspeople will probably have competed at these levels as they have risen in their sport:

- local level (for a school team or something similar)

- regional level (for an area team or even a county team)

- national level (in national championships)

- international level (representing their country against other countries).

The organization involved at these different levels is quite considerable. Without the proper backing, no-one would be able to compete at all of these different standards. Clubs, **local authorities**, schools and national **governing bodies** all play their part in helping individuals and teams to participate in their sport.

Running a club: the people

From the most basic level to the highest, clubs have a particular structure which they follow, so that they can run efficiently and enable sport to take place. Not all clubs are **professional**, run by people who are paid to work for them full-time. Many of them, especially at the lower levels, are run by volunteers who do all of the work in their spare time. They each have particular jobs to do.

In almost any club, the following people would be taking responsibilities:

- The **chairperson** has overall control of the club and runs any regular club meetings. These meetings are governed by a set of rules called the club's **constitution** and the chairperson makes sure that these rules are followed. This is the most senior **official** within the club. The chairperson would represent the club at any other meetings.

The Royal & Ancient Golf Club at St Andrews, Scotland, was founded in 1754.

Officials of a small club discussing club business.

- The **vice-chairperson** (VC) deputizes for the chairperson if they are unable to do their job for some reason. The VC may have to run meetings and often needs to be available at short notice. If the chairperson is very busy, the VC will help by carrying out some of the duties.

- The **secretary** does a very important job in any club, and has to deal with most of the written work. The secretary may have to write and answer letters and emails, and keep the minutes (the record of what went on) of all the club's meetings. This is usually one of the busiest and most demanding jobs, especially in a big club. If a club can afford to pay any of their officials, it is usually the secretary who is paid, as the job is so demanding.

- The **treasurer** deals with all the financial affairs of the club. This person would probably have to run a bank account on behalf of the club. This account is used to pay bills, bank the **subscriptions** taken and ensure that the club has enough money to pay for equipment or the hire of facilities.

- **Committee members** are people who are elected by the members to manage the club. They have regular meetings where they take decisions on behalf of the club and ensure that it runs smoothly. There are often quite a lot of sub-committees within a club for such areas as team selection, fund-raising or even discipline.

- **Members** are all the people who join a club. You cannot hold any of the other positions within the club unless you are a member. You usually pay a fee or subscription to belong to the club. The members usually have the right to have a say in how the club should be run. They are all entitled to go to the Annual General Meeting (AGM), where the officials of the club are elected for the forthcoming year.

Open days can encourage people to try out a new sport.

What clubs do

All the clubs that exist, at any of the different levels, perform their own particular functions:

- *Providing facilities* – a sports club must have somewhere where the members can play their sport. Sometimes, if it is a big club, it may own its own facilities – as would be the case with a golf club. Many smaller clubs hire or rent the facilities where they play. These clubs need to decide when and how the facilities could be used, and there is usually some kind of booking system that they would manage.

- *Organization of competitions and events* – this is one of the main functions of a sports club, and a variety of different types of competition would be included. The club is likely to play competitively against other clubs and at different levels. However, the clubs also have to cater for those members who just want to play for fun or for their own personal pleasure and who do not particularly want to compete.

- *Promotion of their sport* – this can take many forms. The club will need to promote its particular sport, so that it can continue to attract members. The clubs may have **open days**, where anyone is invited to come along and join in. They may also have **taster sessions**, where people are given some basic instruction in the sport and offered an opportunity to try it out.

- *Encouragement for juniors* – many clubs have a junior or youth section, which caters specifically for young players. Every club needs to get young players involved, to ensure that it will keep going and prosper in the future. Some clubs may even adapt their particular sport to suit young players; short tennis played at tennis clubs is a good example of this.

- *Community status and involvement* – all clubs, from large professional ones through to small local ones, can help by being involved in the local community. By getting people involved in trying out or taking part in sport, they may attract them as supporters or spectators, and this may lead to new members joining. Many professional football clubs attract tens of thousands of supporters to their games. This encourages a large part of the community to be united behind the club.

Professional clubs

These clubs are run as businesses and they are usually privately owned. This means that they are not run in the same way as small, local sports clubs. They may well have the same types of officials, but these will be employed full-time and will be paid for their services. Professional sports clubs are usually led by a **chief executive** or managing director. The players, or people who take part in the sport, will probably also be full-time paid professionals who make their living out of playing their sport.

Local authorities

All local authorities, such as local and regional councils, have a duty to make provision for sport and recreation in their area. This means they may provide coaching courses as well as the basic facilities for people to play and take part in sport. They usually do this through:

• school and educational facilities

• leisure centres.

All schools must have some sports facilities, so that Physical Education (P.E.) can be taught. It is one of the subjects that, by law, *must* be taught within a school. This often results in there being an arrangement for **dual use** or **dual provision** (joint provision) so that these facilities can be used by others:

• *dual use* means that the school has the use of the facilities during the day and at other times they are available for public use.

• *dual provision* means that the facilities are jointly used and owned; the public and the school may even be sharing them at the same time.

Anyone can use facilities with dual use and dual provision.

School organization

For the majority of young people, school is the main place where they play sports. This is because sport is compulsory, so every pupil takes part. In addition, many schools provide **extra-curricular activities**, which take place outside of the normal time-tabled lessons. These usually include extra sporting activities. They may take place during the lunch-time breaks or, more commonly, after school has finished in the afternoons. Some are even held during the weekends.

Some schools have built up a tradition for holding regular sporting fixtures, for example on Wednesday afternoons and on Saturday mornings. This can lead to many ex-pupils continuing to play sport together. They may even form their own teams and compete as 'former pupils'.

However, not all schools can provide a full range of extra-curricular activities, so it is important that they establish links with other organizations that can.

Sporting links

Clubs are very keen to encourage young people to join. One of the best ways for clubs to get young people interested in sport – and to keep them interested – is by forming strong links with schools.

A club may be able to provide extra coaching in activities already offered by the school. Alternatively, the club could give opportunities in a completely different activity, which the school is unable to offer because it lacks the facilities, staff expertise, time or specialist equipment. A strong link between clubs and schools benefits both because:

• the clubs will be keen to keep their standards up;

• the schools' pupils are able to have extra practice and training.

Many professional clubs (especially football clubs) even send **scouts** to schools to watch matches and invite the young players to join them. These scouts are members of the club

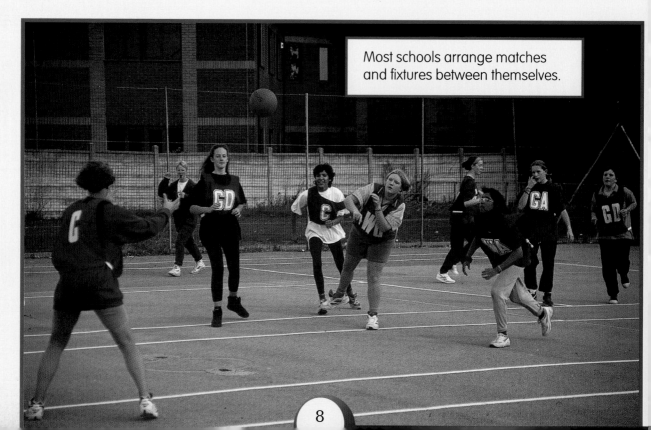

Most schools arrange matches and fixtures between themselves.

staff whose job it is to find, and sign, talented youngsters. In recent years, many national governing bodies and professional clubs have set up youth academies, to attract and assist talented young players. If a club can get talented players to join them when they are young, they don't need to spend vast amounts of money buying players from other clubs in the future. This is why many clubs have youth policies and run several youth teams made up of local young players.

Encouraging young people to continue to take an active part in sport has been a priority for many years. Research has shown that young people quickly lose interest in sport when they leave school and stop taking part in it. This pattern of behaviour is known as the **Wolfendon Gap** (named after the writer of an important report).

Schools are greatly encouraged to form strong links with clubs in their area. This is so young people can continue to take part in sport after they leave school and also have access to more sporting opportunities. There was a time when young people could not continue with an activity because the only facilities were in the schools and they could not use them once they had left.

The role of national governing bodies

Each of the various sports is run by its own national governing body. Although these bodies do not actually manage their sport at all levels, they do make the rules and issue the guidelines that all of the regional and local organizations have to follow. They decide on:

- finance

- fixtures

- discipline

- coaching

- promotion and advertising.

The majority of people who help with the organization of sport do so as volunteers. In the governing bodies, there are paid officials in the most responsible jobs.

Governing bodies

There are about 270 governing bodies of sport in the UK alone. Just about every sport you could think of has one!

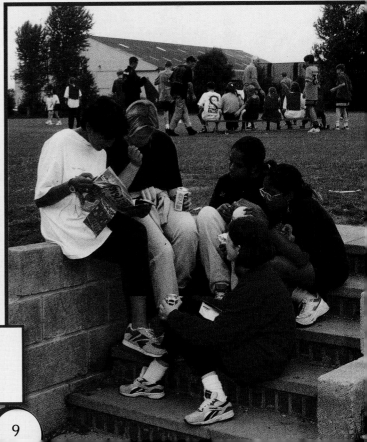

Not all young people actively take part in sport. But sport is encouraged as part of a healthy lifestyle.

2 Competitions

Most sport is competitive. For many people this is an important reason why they like to play it. However, the type of competition in each sport has to be carefully selected and it must be well organized. Competitions may take the form of:

- knockouts
- leagues
- round robins
- ladders.

Clubs may use any or all of the above **competition formats**, for fairness and to attract players' and supporters' interest.

The Wimbledon Championship is a knockout competition in which the top players are seeded.

Knockouts

These competitions are very popular. They are often used when there is a very large number of people or teams taking part, because it is the quickest and easiest type of competition to organize.

The event is always played in rounds. This means that each team plays against one other team and the winner then goes through to the next round. The number of teams taking part is halved in each round, as the losing teams drop out. This is the main disadvantage of this type of competition: some teams only get to compete once. The second best team in the entire competition could get knocked out in the very first round and a less skilful team could get to the final!

To avoid this, many competitions have seeded teams or players. This means the organizers spread out the best players or teams throughout the draw for the competition, so that the two top ones can only meet if they both get through to the final. The Wimbledon tennis championship

Knockout competitions

In most sports, at least one knockout competition is organized because the format is very exciting and it generates a lot of interest from supporters and the media. It is rare for any team to win all the knockout and league competitions of their sport. To win both a knockout and a league is known as a 'double'.

is organized along these lines. However, it does depend upon the organizers taking the right decisions about who the best players are! They use computer software that keeps a constant and updated record of all of the players' performances, and then gives them a **ranking position**.

Another way of organizing a competition is to have preliminary rounds, where less skilful teams play against each other for the right to play against the top teams or players in the later rounds. This method is often used in football competitions, because the game is very popular and large numbers of teams and players want to take part. It happens in the football **World Cup** (which is played in qualifying groups) and also in the Football Association Cup (the FA Cup). Most of the international competitions in any sport start with a qualifying stage and end with a knockout stage.

Organizing a knockout competition can be very complicated because you need rounds with possibly 128, 64, 32, 16, 8, 4 and finally 2 players or teams. You must always 'knock out' half the teams or players, in every round. You may not always have the right number of entries for this system but the competition will not work any other way! The solution to the problem of having too few entries is to have a preliminary round with byes (some of the teams or players do not take part). Then you end up with the right numbers for your proper first round.

So that teams or players can have further opportunities to play when they have been knocked out in the first round, some knockout competitions organize a **plate competition**. All of the first round losers take part in another knockout competition, which is again played up to a final. This at least guarantees all of the players at least two games and keeps up interest in the competition.

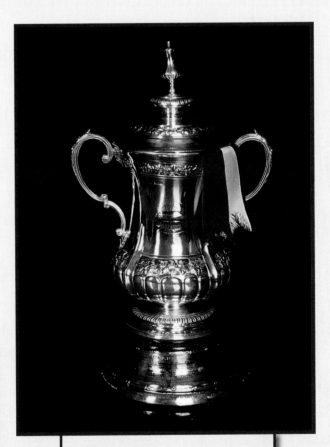

The FA Cup is one of the oldest knockout competitions.

FA Cup stages

When the final stages of one year's FA Cup are taking place, some teams are already involved in the preliminary stages of the next season's competition!

Leagues

This is a very common and popular type of competition. It is usually considered to be the hardest to win, and therefore the most important. A league usually takes place over a long period of time. It rewards the most consistent team or player, who as a result manages to finish up at the top of the league.

Most sports have a particular **season** when they are played. The league competition will run throughout this season. A league competition is well-suited to include a large number of teams, or entries, as it gives them all a chance to play. It also makes sure that they have plenty of games. Each team plays against each of the others at least once. Often they play twice, once at home and once away. The teams get points for winning or drawing games or matches. They do not usually get any points at all if they lose a match!

Because there may be a large number of teams wishing to take part in one particular sport, the leagues may be split up into several divisions.

English football leagues

Professional football in England is the largest organized league in the country, with a total of 92 professional teams included in all of the divisions. Each season they all play against each other. The teams in the Premier League try to finish top of their league, to be the best team in the country and to qualify for European competition. Other clubs can also qualify for Europe by finishing high in the Premier League or winning the League and Football Association knockout competitions.

The teams at the bottom of the Premier League have to try to avoid being **relegated** to a lower division. Within the other leagues there are many teams trying to be **promoted** to the higher divisions, and many trying not to be relegated to the lower divisions. The very bottom teams of the lowest division actually have to drop out of the Football League altogether and are replaced by teams from the **Conference**. There is a whole set of other leagues below the Football League, and they have their own promotion and relegation arrangements.

Scotland has a similar arrangement of national leagues and divisions to England, though fewer of the players outside the Scottish Premier League are full-time professionals. Northern Ireland has a smaller set of leagues. In Wales, there is only one national league division, with the rest arranged on a local basis.

Many players start their careers in the lower leagues, where a lot of the players are **semi-professional** (they have jobs as well as getting paid for playing football). They try to work their way up through the system until they end up playing for one of the top professional clubs. This system can also work in reverse. As players grow older, they often drop down divisions and may play at lower levels towards the end of their careers.

Some of the many advantages to organizing activities on a league basis are that:

- fixtures can be arranged in advance and publicized;

- a certain number of games are guaranteed to be played;

- tickets (and season tickets) can be sold a long time in advance;

- it is the most profitable system over a long period of time, in terms of finance.

Football Details, Scorers and Tables

FA CUP

(sponsored by Littlewoods)

Fourth round

BLACKBURN ....(1) 1 COVENTRY ......(2) 2
Sherwood 1 — Jess 28, Huckerby 44 — 21,123

Coventry away to Derby on Wednesday February 26, 7.45

Fifth round

BIRMINGHAM ..(1) 1 WREXHAM ......(0) 3
Bruce 37 — Hughes 51, Humes 61, Connolly 90 — 21,511

CHESTERFIELD .(0) 1 NOTTM F ....(0) 0
Curtis 54 (pen) — 8,890

LEEDS ....(0) 2 PORTSMOUTH ...(1) 3
Bowyer 52, 90 — McLoughlin 7, Svensson 67, Bradbury 86 — 35,604

MAN CITY ......(0) 0 MIDDLESBRO .....(0) 1
Juninho 77 — 30,462

WIMBLEDON ...(1) 2 Q.P.R. ....(1) 1
Gayle 44, Earle 55 — Hateley 41 — 22,395

■ THE draw for the sixth round will take place today at approximately 6pm and be broadcast live on BBC1 TV and BBC Radio Five Live.

FA CARLING PREMIERSHIP

DERBY ....(0) 1 WEST HAM ......(0) 0
Asanovic 53 (pen) — 18,057

TOTTENHAM ...(0) 0 ARSENAL ....(0) 0
33,039

		Home					Away					
	P	W	D	L	F	A	W	D	L	F	A	Pts
Man Utd	25	9	3	1	26	10	5	5	2	24	18	50
Liverpool	25	7	5	1	26	10	7	2	3	16	10	49
Arsenal	26	8	4	0	29	11	5	5	4	15	12	48
Newcastle	25	9	2	2	38	16	4	4	4	12	14	45
Chelsea	24	6	5	1	22	14	5	3	4	16	19	41
Wimbledon	23	6	4	1	20	12	5	2	5	16	16	39
Aston Villa	25	7	3	3	19	10	4	3	5	13	15	39
Sheff Wed	24	4	7	1	11	8	4	4	4	15	19	35
Tottenham	25	5	4	5	15	14	4	1	6	12	19	32
Everton	25	5	2	5	19	14	3	5	5	15	24	31
Leeds	25	5	3	5	12	12	3	3	6	9	15	30
Sunderland	25	5	5	2	13	8	2	3	8	10	24	29
Derby	25	5	3	4	12	11	1	7	5	11	19	28
Blackburn	24	5	2	4	15	11	1	7	5	11	14	27
Leicester	24	4	3	5	12	17	3	3	6	13	18	27
Coventry	25	3	4	5	12	15	3	5	5	11	18	27
Nottm F	25	3	5	5	11	18	2	3	7	12	22	23
West Ham	25	4	3	6	13	17	1	4	7	7	16	22
Southampton	23	4	3	4	20	13	1	2	9	12	28	20
†Middlesbro	24	4	4	4	21	18	1	3	8	9	26	19

† 3pts deducted

SE COUNTIES — Cambridge 1 Norwich 2; Chelsea 2 West Ham 1; Gillingham 3 Ipswich 3; Millwall 1 Arsenal 3; QPR 1 L Orient 0; Tottenham 2 Charlton 0. Div 2: Barnet 1 Bristol R 1; C Palace 6 Tottenham 2; Oxford 2 Luton 2; Wimbledon 1 Colchester 2; Wycombe 2 Reading 0.

PONTINS — Prem: Liverpool 2 Tranmere 1.

NATIONWIDE DIVISION ONE

BOLTON ....(2) 2 SHEFF UTD ......(1) 2
Paatelainen 4, Fairclough 20 — Fjortoft 7, Katchouro 55 — 17,922

CHARLTON ......(1) 2 BARNSLEY ......(0) 2
Nicholls 1, Lee 88 — Hendrie 48, 90 — 9,104

GRIMSBY ....(1) 2 HUDDERSFIELD ..(1) 2
Widdrington 5, Lester 57 — Stewart 44, Edwards 48 — 6,197

NORWICH ......(0) 2 WEST BROM .....(1) 4
Sutch 65, Adams 78 (pen) — Peschisolido 9, 56, 68, Sneekes 49 — 14,845

OXFORD ....(2) 3 OLDHAM ....(0) 1
Graham 34 (og), Purse 42, Jemson 89 — Graham 72 — 6,868

PORT VALE .....(2) 2 IPSWICH ....(1) 2
Mills 40, Porter 43 (pen) — Mason 9, Stockwell 69 — 6,115

SOUTHEND .....(1) 2 STOKE ....(0) 1
Thomson 34, Rammell 89 — Harris 70 (og) — 4,625

WOLVES ....(0) 0 C PALACE ....(1) 3
Tuttle 17, Veart 72, Dyer 73 — 25,919

		Home					Away					
	P	W	D	L	F	A	W	D	L	F	A	Pts
Bolton	33	12	4	1	38	16	6	7	3	31	28	65
Barnsley	31	9	3	3	29	14	6	7	3	24	23	55
Wolves	32	7	3	7	20	17	9	4	2	24	14	55
Sheff Utd	32	7	5	4	30	19	7	4	5	24	19	51
C Palace	31	7	3	4	28	14	6	7	4	31	19	49
Norwich	32	7	7	3	22	15	7	0	8	24	33	49
Stoke	31	10	1	4	23	17	3	6	7	17	26	46
Ipswich	32	7	6	2	28	17	4	6	7	17	24	45
Portsmouth	32	8	3	5	21	16	5	3	8	17	21	45
Port Vale	33	4	9	4	26	23	6	5	5	14	15	44
Oxford	32	10	3	3	30	14	2	4	10	15	27	43
Q.P.R.	32	6	4	6	22	19	5	6	5	22	26	43
Tranmere	31	8	4	4	31	22	4	3	8	12	20	43
Swindon	32	8	5	3	31	17	4	1	11	14	25	42
West Brom	33	3	7	6	26	26	6	7	4	28	32	41
Huddersfield	33	8	4	4	23	14	2	7	8	16	32	41
Charlton	31	7	5	4	23	19	4	1	10	12	24	39
Reading	31	8	6	2	26	18	1	4	10	14	30	37
Birmingham	29	7	4	3	20	12	2	6	7	12	21	37
Man City	30	7	3	5	20	16	3	2	10	16	27	35
Southend	32	6	6	4	24	22	1	5	10	6	34	32
Grimsby	31	4	5	8	21	30	3	5	6	19	25	31
Bradford	32	6	5	5	18	22	1	5	10	12	27	31
Oldham	30	3	5	6	14	19	3	5	8	17	22	28

SMIRNOFF IRISH — Prem: Cliftonville 2 Ards 1; Coleraine 3 Crusaders 1; Glentoran 0 Linfield 2; Portadown 1 Glenavon 1. Div I: Ballyclare 2 Carrick 0; Bangor 1 Newry 2; Distillery 0 Larne 0; Omagh 0 Ballymena 4.

WESTWARD DEVELOPMENTS DEVON — Appledore A A C 5 Newton St Cyres 1; Elburton 2 Cullompton 1; Ottery St Mary 1 Buckfastleigh 4; Plymouth Command 5 Ivybridge 2; Teignmouth 0 Topsham 5; Weston Mill Oak Villa 6 Alphington 1; Willand 4 Plymstock 0.

GERMANY — Duisburg 1 Bochum 1; Bayern Munich 3 St Pauli 0; Schalke 1 Stuttgart 0; Karlsruhe 1 Hansa Rostock 1; Werder Bremen 1 Freiburg 0; Hamburg 2 1860 Munich 3.

DIVISION TWO

BOURNEMOUTH (0) 0 BURNLEY ....(0) 0
6,021

BRISTOL R ......(1) 3 LUTON ....(1) 2
Miller 22, Tillson 47, Holloway 54 — Thorpe 10 (pen), Waddock 64 — 5,612

CREWE ....(0) 1 WALSALL ....(0) 0
Murphy 47 — 4,648

MILLWALL ......(0) 2 ROTHERHAM ....(0) 0
Crawford 81, Gayle 90 (og) — 7,043

NOTTS CO ......(1) 1 BLACKPOOL .....(1) 1
Butler 28 (og) — Quinn 4 — 5,281

PETERBOROUGH (1) 3 BRISTOL CITY ....(0) 1
Willis 16, 85, Otto 90 — Barnard 82 (pen) — 4,221

PLYMOUTH .....(0) 2 BURY ....(0) 0
Logan 63, Corazzin 66 — 5,486

PRESTON ......(1) 2 WYCOMBE ....(1) 1
McKenna 15, Davey 82 — McGavin 25 — 7,923

STOCKPORT ....(0) 3 SHREWSBURY ...(0) 1
Angell 75, 76, Armstrong 87 — Whiston 60 — 6,712

YORK ....(1) 2 GILLINGHAM ....(1) 3
Bushell 23, Barras 79 — Onuora 4, Ratcliffe 67, Akinbiyi 84 — 2,748

		Home					Away					
	P	W	D	L	F	A	W	D	L	F	A	Pts
Brentford	30	6	9	0	24	14	9	2	4	24	15	56
Luton	29	10	3	2	27	8	5	4	5	22	24	52
Crewe	30	12	1	2	30	8	4	1	10	12	25	50
Bristol City	31	9	4	3	32	13	4	5	6	17	21	48
Stockport	29	8	4	3	21	11	5	5	4	21	21	48
Bury	28	9	4	0	23	6	4	5	6	18	23	48
Millwall	31	10	2	4	23	16	3	6	6	17	24	47
Burnley	32	11	1	5	33	19	2	6	7	12	17	46
Chesterfield	28	7	4	2	14	9	6	3	6	11	11	46
Wrexham	28	7	5	1	24	17	4	7	4	12	14	45
Walsall	30	9	4	2	23	11	4	2	9	13	21	45
Watford	28	5	7	2	13	10	5	8	1	16	11	45
Bournemouth	34	6	5	6	16	16	5	4	8	15	20	42
Shrewsbury	32	7	5	5	22	22	3	4	8	20	29	39
Blackpool	30	6	6	2	25	13	3	6	7	13	19	39
Preston	32	8	4	4	21	16	3	2	11	11	22	39
Gillingham	31	7	3	5	23	18	3	5	8	12	23	38
Bristol R	31	8	4	3	25	17	1	6	9	7	17	37
Plymouth	31	5	8	3	16	16	3	4	8	19	28	36
York	31	5	3	7	18	22	4	3	9	14	28	33
Peterborough	31	4	6	6	29	26	3	5	7	14	27	32
Wycombe	30	7	2	6	15	13	1	4	10	14	30	30
Notts Co	31	3	6	6	14	16	2	4	10	9	24	25
Rotherham	30	4	5	7	13	17	0	4	10	11	30	21

JEWSON SW — Liskeard 0 Torpoint 0; Newquay 1 Millbrook 1; Porthleven 3 St Austell 0; Wadebridge 2 Saltash 0; Tavistock 1 Penzance 1; Launceston 0 Holsworthy 3; Falmouth 2 St Blazey 1. Cup qtr-final replay: Truro 2 Bodmin 0.

SKURRAYS WILTS — Devizes Res 4 Wroughton 1; Purton Res 2 Corsham 3; Southbrook Wal 2 Aldbourne 2; Tisbury 2 Burmah Cas 1.

CLUBSAVER HANTS — AFC Newbury 6 Winchester Cty 0; Blackfield &L 5 New Milton 0; Hayling 1 Fleetlands 1; Horndean 3 Overton 0; Netley Cen 1 Bass Alton 0; Poole 2 Colden Cmn 4. Div 2: Hedge End 2 Ringwood 4; Hythe &D 2 Brading 3; Ludgershall 0 Esso 2; Vosper Thorn 1 Verwood 2.

DIVISION THREE

CARLISLE ......(2) 2 BRIGHTON ......(1) 1
Smart 24, Walling 35 — Maskell 43 — 5,465

DARLINGTON ...(1) 2 SCUNTHORPE ...(0) 0
Naylor 3, Twynham 86 — 2,245

DONCASTER ....(1) 1 BARNET ....(0) 1
Moore 28 — Ndah 47 — 2,199

FULHAM ....(0) 1 WIGAN ....(0) 1
Blake 82 (pen) — Lowe 52 — 9,448

HARTLEPOOL ...(1) 1 TORQUAY ....(0) 1
Beech 38 — Jack 64 — 1,548

HULL ....(2) 2 EXETER ....(0) 0
Joyce 7, Gordon 22 — 2,668

LEYTON O ......(0) 1 CAMBRIDGE .....(1) 1
McGleish 59 — Taylor 21 — 4,418

MANSFIELD ....(2) 2 LINCOLN ....(0) 2
Martindale 6, Sedgemore 42 — Ainsworth 73, Stant 75 — 3,037

ROCHDALE .....(1) 1 NORTHAMPTON .(1) 1
Deary 44 — Rush 9 — 1,988

SWANSEA ......(1) 1 SCARBOROUGH ..(0) 2
Penney 4 (pen) — Bennett 48, Williams 86 — 3,312

		Home					Away					
	P	W	D	L	F	A	W	D	L	F	A	Pts
Fulham	33	10	3	4	32	17	9	3	4	24	15	63
Carlisle	31	12	2	2	27	13	6	6	3	19	15	62
Wigan	31	11	1	2	30	13	7	5	5	25	23	60
Swansea	34	10	3	4	26	12	6	3	8	18	25	54
Cambridge	32	10	2	3	24	15	6	4	7	19	25	54
Colchester	33	8	8	1	29	15	4	8	4	19	19	52
Scarborough	33	7	7	3	24	19	5	5	6	22	22	48
Northampton	32	10	3	4	34	14	3	5	7	17	21	47
Cardiff	31	8	1	7	24	20	6	3	6	15	19	46
Chester	31	7	5	3	23	12	5	5	6	13	19	46
Lincoln	33	7	7	3	23	17	5	2	9	23	35	45
Mansfield	32	5	6	5	15	13	5	7	4	20	19	43
Hull	32	7	6	3	20	17	3	7	6	10	16	43
Torquay	31	9	2	5	18	11	3	4	8	14	23	42
Leyton O	34	8	6	3	20	11	2	5	10	11	22	41
Scunthorpe	30	8	1	7	29	26	3	4	7	14	21	38
Hartlepool	33	5	6	6	24	26	5	1	10	13	23	37
Rochdale	31	6	5	4	21	16	2	8	6	15	23	37
Barnet	31	5	7	3	20	13	3	6	7	10	18	37
Darlington	32	7	4	5	28	20	2	3	11	17	38	34
Hereford	32	5	4	7	20	18	4	2	10	15	30	33
Exeter	33	5	5	6	16	17	3	3	11	13	29	32
Doncaster	32	5	4	6	17	17	3	2	12	17	38	30
*Brighton	33	6	5	5	27	20	1	2	14	9	33	26

** 2pts deducted*

DORSET COMB — Allendale 2 Bournemouth Spt 3; Blandford 5 Bridport 0; Flight Ref 4 Westland Spt 0; Gillingham 2 Weymouth Spt 2; Hamworth 1 Swanage T & H 1; Portland 5 Parley Spt 1; Sherborne 1 Dorchester 3; Sturminster Marsh 2 Shaftesbury 1; Wareham 2 Sturminster New 2.

SCHOOLS — FA Prem U-16 Trophy: Bedfordshire 1 Inner London 1. English Knowles Cup: Norfolk 2 Suffolk 1. Miller Trophy: Vale of White Horse 3 Slough 2. Yorkshire Trophy: Hull 2 Leeds 5. Finch Trophy: Newham 0 Barking 0. Smeathers Trophy: Havering 4 SE Sussex 0. Snowdon Cup: Liverpool 2 Halton 1. Merseyside Cup: Sefton 7 St Helens 0.

FULL DETAILS FROM THE FOOTBALL PYRAMID

GM VAUXHALL CONFERENCE

DOVER ....(1) 2 BROMSGRVE ....(0) 0
Strouts 17, Brown 73 — 1,023

FARNBORO .....(1) 1 STALYBRIDGE ...(0) 0
Wingfield 8 — 696

GATESHEAD ....(0) 0 HEDNESFORD ...(0) 1
O'Connor 68 — 694

HALIFAX ......(2) 4 BATH ....(3) 5
Horsfield 15, 81, Lyons 32, Martin 71 — Harrington 31, Davis 41, 82, Brooks 43, Colbourne 86 — 655

KIDD'MNSTR ...(1) 1 ALTRINCHAM ...(0) 1
Hughes 42 — McGoona 85 — 2,679

MACCLESFLD ...(1) 2 RUSHDEN ....(1) 1
Wood 37, Byrne 65 — Leworthy 35 — 1,304

MORECAMBE ...(1) 1 WELLING ....(1) 2
Copley 17 (og) — Holden 10 (og), Dennis 84 — 877

SLOUGH ....(2) 3 NORTHWICH ....(2) 4
Brazil 27, Clement 32, Barclay 74 — Vicary 24, Cooke 37, 64, 89 — 703

STEVENAGE ....(0) 0 KETTERING ......(0) 0
2,864

TELFORD ....(0) 0 HAYES ....(0) 0
812

WOKING ....(0) 0 SOUTHPORT ....(1) 1
Howard 34 (og) — 2,858

		Home					Away					
	P	W	D	L	F	A	W	D	L	F	A	Pts
Kidd'mnstr	30	11	3	3	39	16	8	3	2	23	9	63
Macclesfld	30	10	3	2	22	8	8	4	3	22	9	61
Northwich	30	9	3	3	22	12	5	5	5	20	25	50
Stevenage	26	9	3	1	34	14	5	3	5	18	18	48
Hednesford	26	7	4	2	18	6	6	3	4	18	18	46
Morecambe	27	7	2	4	24	15	6	3	5	24	20	44
Farnboro	26	6	4	4	25	21	6	4	2	16	9	44
Woking	26	7	4	3	30	17	4	4	4	17	17	41
Telford	32	5	6	6	18	25	6	2	7	18	22	41
Southport	26	6	3	4	18	17	5	4	4	16	17	40
Slough	31	6	5	6	37	26	4	3	7	13	22	38
Stalybridge	29	7	2	5	24	16	4	3	8	14	22	38
Welling	25	6	2	4	16	15	3	5	5	19	24	34
Altrincham	28	5	2	7	15	19	3	7	4	18	27	33
Kettering	27	4	4	3	16	11	4	3	9	16	26	31
Dover	29	5	6	3	21	21	2	4	9	16	30	31
Gateshead	28	3	4	7	20	21	4	4	6	17	24	29
Hayes	28	5										
Bromsgrove	30	5										
Halifax	26	5										
Bath	31	5										
Rushden	27	3										

SCREWFIX DIRE

DR MARTENS PREMIER

ASHFORD TOWN (0) 1 GRESLEY ....(1) 3
Wynter 54 — Hurst 10, Garner 65 (pen), Marsden 75 — 615

BURTON ....(0) 1 GRAVESEND & N .(3) 3
Marlow 55 — Robinson 4, 28, Lovell 30 — 713

CHELT'NHAM ..(0) 1 CHELMSFORD ...(0) 0
Wright 63 — 763

CRAWLEY ....P NUNEATON ....P

DORCHESTER ...(1) 3 KING'S LYNN ....(0) 0
Wilkinson 30, Pickard 55, 59 — 638

GLOUCESTER ...(0) 2 HASTINGS ....(0) 0
Tucker 73, Watkins 86 — 612

HALESOWEN ...(2) 6 BALDOCK ....(0) 0
Wright 5, 52, 72 (pen), 89, Bellingham 19, Coates 74 — 681

MERTHYR T .....(0) 1 SUDBURY ....(1) 3
Summers 83 — Stock 45, Pope 49, Brown 90 — 505

NEWPORT ......(0) 0 CAMBRIDGE .....(0) 0
560

SALISBURY .....(2) 3 ATHERSTONE ....(0) 2
Chalk 43, Evans 45, Lovell 58 — Percival 86, Ellison 90 — 284

SITTINGBRNE ...(0) 0 WORCESTER ....(0) 1
Thomas 81 — 537

		Home					Away					
	P	W	D	L	F	A	W	D	L	F	A	Pts
Gresley	26	6	5	2	22	13	10	3	0	27	12	56
Halesowen	28	7	5	2	29	17	8	2	4	26	15	52
King's Lynn	28	9	2	3	25	16	5	5	4	19	21	49
Cheltenham	26	9	1	5	24	13	6	2	3	25	15	48
Gloucester	27	10	1	3	28	18	5	2	6	22	16	48
Burton	28	6	5	3	23	17	6	2	6	22	22	43
Sudbury	23	8	0	2	23	11	5	3	5	24	23	42
Merthyr T	27	8	2	5	25	16	4	4	4	19	21	42
Worcester	28	7	4	3	24	16	3	5	6	16	21	39
Nuneaton	27	8	1	4	25	17	3	5	6	8	17	39
Graves'd & N	28	8	2	4	25	19	3	3	8	17	28	38
Salisbury	24	5	3	4	17	17	5	4	3	20	17	37
Sittingbrne	27	4	3	7	22	26	5	3	5	24	22	33
Atherstone	27	4	7	4	15	19	3	2	7	15	18	30
Dorchester	24	6	2	6	24	22	2	3	5	11	16	29

ICIS PREMIER

AYLESBURY ....(1) 3 GRAYS ....(0) 0
Swaysland 30, 61, Davies 60 — 554

BISHOPS ST ....(1) 2 HENDON ....(1) 1
Cooper 11, 83 — Dawber 32 — 476

BOREHAM WD ..(2) 3 CARSHALTON ...(0) 0
Liburd 41 (pen), Robbins 45, Prutton 64 — 219

ENFIELD ....(2) 5 CHERTSEY ......(0) 0
Arron 13 (pen), Edwards 44, May, 47, 66, Tucker 78 — 714

HARROW ....(0) 3 HITCHIN ....(0) 1
James 50, Hooper 59, Butler 81 — Dellar 46 — 220

HEYBRIDGE .....(0) 1 DULWICH ....(1) 1
Keen 40 — Chin 6 — 305

PURFLEET ......(1) 2 OXFORD CITY ....(1) 2
Williams 8, Cobb 66 — Matlock 7, Greig 83 — 179

STAINES ....(0) 0 DAG-REDBGE ....(0) 0
265

SUTTON UTD ...(1) 2 ST ALBANS ......(2) 3
Coleman 39 (og), Hynes 61 — Clark 2, Cobb 6 (pen), Daly 54 — 579

YEADING ....(1) 1 BROMLEY ....(0) 0
Kenman 14 — 160

YEOVIL ....(1) 2 KINGSTONIAN ...(2) 3
Forinton 31, 85 — Darlington 2, 62, Evans 24 — 2,242

		Home					Away					
	P	W	D	L	F	A	W	D	L	F	A	Pts
Enfield	25	9	2	2	35	14	9	3	0	25	6	59
Yeovil	24	9	1	1	19	6	9	2	2	20	12	57
Sutton Utd	23	8	3	2	32	20	4	4	2	19	17	43
Dulwich	25	7	1	4	22	13	5	5	3	20	16	42
Dag-Redbge	23	8	2	2	24	9	3	6	2	10	7	41
Purfleet	27	6	6	3	24	18	5	1	6	17	18	40
Oxford City	26	6	2	4	25	18	5	5	4	24	27	40
Aylesbury	24	8	3	2	22	14	3	3	5	8	13	39
Yeading	23	5	3	3	18	10	5	4	3	17	15	37
Heybridge	24	6	3	4	17	22	4	2	5	15	19	35
Kingstonian	27	6	3	5	32	25	4	1	8	20	30	34
Carshalton	27	5	4	4	18	13	3	3	8	13	27	31
Bishops St	25	6	4	3	16	11	3	0	9	10	26	31
Boreham Wd	23	5	2	4	19	13	4	1	7	12	21	30

UNIBOND PREMIER

B AUCKLAND ...(0) 1 CHORLEY ....(2) 3
Waller 59 (pen) — Sang 6, Potts 31, Trundle 85 — 211

BARROW ....(0) 1 GUISELEY ....(1) 1
Green 76 — Matthews 12 — 968

BLYTH SP ....(2) 3 RUNCORN ....(0) 2
McGargle 20, 36, 64 — Dunn 60, Ruffer 90 — 520

EMLEY ....(0) 1 BAMBER BR .....(1) 2
Lacey 67 — Woodward 17, Haddock 58 — 212

GAINSBORO' ...(2) 3 WITTON ....(0) 0
Matthews 2, Maxwell 10, Marrow 79 — 383

HYDE ....(4) 7 ACCRINGTON ....(0) 2
Carroll 4, Nolan 18 (pen), Owen 40, 45, Kimmins 61, James 72, 88 — Ormerod 80, 82 — 578

KNOWSLEY .....(0) 0 BOSTON ....(0) 0
90

LEEK ....(3) 3 FRICKLEY ....(0) 0
Fuson 18, Tobin 22, Higginbotham 31 — 417

MARINE ....(2) 3 BUXTON ....(0) 0
McNally 10, Blackhurst 17, Daley 62 — 303

SPENNYMOOR ..(1) 3 ALFRETON TOWN (0) 2
Shaw 26, Cowell 60, Innes 85 — Pickering 47, Walsh 88 — 202

WINSFORD .....(0) 0 LANCASTER .....(1) 1
Diggle 13 — 146

		Home					Away					
	P	W	D	L	F	A	W	D	L	F	A	Pts
Leek	28	10	3	1	27	10	9	2	3	25	14	62
Barrow	34	8	6	3	29	14	9	2	6	25	22	59
Hyde	29	8	6	0	32	14	7	5	3	36	21	56
Boston	27	7	3	1	27	15	7	5	4	22	13	50
Blyth Sp	29	8	4	4	28	15	7	1	5	20	15	50
Guiseley	30	10	2	3	27	13	4	5	6	18	22	49
Marine	28	7	7	1	20	10	5	4	4	14	16	47
Gainsboro'	27	9	1	4	22	8	4	5	4	25	20	45
Emley	28	6	4	4	31	21	6	4	4	20	18	44
Accrington	31	6	2	7	27	30	5	6	5	26	28	41
B Auckland	25	5	5	4	24	18	5	5	1	17	8	40
Chorley	30	6	4	4	28	20	5	2	9	20	25	39
												38
												37
												36
												33
												33
												33
												26

The English 'pyramid' of soccer leagues has changed several times over the years. It can be fascinating to compare the current league tables with results and tables from over ten years ago, like these ones from February 1997.

Round robin

In this type of competition, all of the teams or competitors play against each other once and the most successful are the winners. One of the drawbacks to this type of competition is that it can only be organized for a fairly small number of teams or players, otherwise it would take far too long!

This method is often used for individual or pairs events, in sports such as tennis and squash. There is often some form of qualifying stage, and the round robin is played during the final stages. One example is in tennis, where the top few players

throughout the season are selected to play in a round robin tournament, almost as a form of final championship for the season. This type of tournament is very attractive to stage, because the organizers can guarantee to have all of the top players playing against each other at some time. Then the public can see all of their favourite **match-ups** between players of similar high standards.

One possible drawback to a straight round robin is that there may be no outright winner, if no one wins all of their games. For this reason, there is usually a **play-off** final at the end between the top two teams or players.

Ladders

Ladders are often thought to be more 'social' or friendly competitions, as they tend to be played in clubs where there is not so much at stake in winning or losing.

All of the players have their names listed on a long 'ladder'. The idea is for one person to challenge people who are above them on the ladder to games, and then to take their place in that higher position if they win. There are usually rules about who can be challenged, depending on how much higher up the ladder they are. For example, the bottom player could not challenge the player at the very top. They would have to work their way up the ladder over quite a long period of time.

This system should end up with the best player at the club being at the top of the ladder. Then the other players would be trying to improve their position.

One of the main drawbacks to this system is that it does not encourage good new players to join in. This is because it may take them a very long time to work their way to the top of the ladder.

Many squash clubs use the ladder system.

Combined competitions

No one type of competition is perfect. Many sports organizations decide to use a combination of several types of competition when running a tournament. Whatever type is used, there will always be claims that it is unfair in one way or another, so a combination is often thought to be best. The main aims of a competition should be to:

• have as many games as possible;

• give teams more than one chance to qualify or win;

• allow as many teams as possible to play against each other, especially where this helps to develop the sport in new countries;

• allow the overall best team or player to win in the end.

Nearly all international sport competitions start off on a league basis, usually in regions. The football World Cup is a good example of this. There may even be competitions among groups of countries or in continents. The winners go on to the final stages. Teams or players who qualify may then play in leagues again, or even in round robin competitions, before getting to the final stages.

Whatever type of competition the organizers choose, there usually has to be a knockout stage as the ultimate final. This is because:

• there is more tension and excitement in **head-to-head** finals;

• leagues can be won and decided before all of the games are played, which **de-motivates** teams and players and leads to an anti-climax;

• these are far more attractive propositions to the **media** (television, press and radio);

• time restrictions may dictate that there has to be a particular winner at one particular time, so holding replays or re-staging events is not possible.

These Italian players are celebrating winning the FIFA World Cup in Germany in 2006. Italy beat France 5-3 on penalties, after a 1-1 draw in normal and extra time. The World Cup has a long period of qualifying, league and knockout stages.

3) Officials

No sporting event can be run properly without **officials** to take responsibility in almost every area. In a top tennis tournament such as Wimbledon you would need up to twelve officials for each of the games that take place and there would be several of these going on at the same time!

The officials at Wimbledon would include the **umpire** and all of the **line judges** as well as the **net cord judge**. For some other sporting events you may need even more than that! All major athletic events need officials for all of the track and field events, and many of the officials need specialist knowledge to do their job properly.

At most activities the officials have very important roles, as they have to organize the competitors and maintain the smooth running of the event or tournament. Very few officials are paid to do their jobs. Many of them are volunteers and only claim their travelling expenses for attending the activity.

In **professional** sports there are more full-time paid officials at the highest levels. There are two main reasons for this:

• the standards and rewards are high and the players and supporters demand the highest standards from the officials;

• the sports events raise enough money to be able to pay the officials.

In most **amateur** sports events or activities played at lower levels, none of the officials are paid. There is simply not enough money because the events do not attract sponsorship or money from tickets.

Some activities and events require a lot of specialist officials.

In most amateur sporting events, there will be the bare minimum of officials. It is quite common for team **members** to take on the role. For example, in many football matches the substitutes act as assistant referees and in cricket matches it is common practice for players to take turns to umpire. In many sports it is not easy to get officials at all and it can be very difficult to get fully **qualified** ones.

Qualifying as an official

It takes quite a long time to qualify as an official in any recognized sporting activity. Training usually means going on a course, which has to be paid for. The training has to be recognized by the **governing body** of that sport, which will often arrange it as well. It can take quite a long time to work up through all of the different levels, as all officials are expected to be experienced at lower levels before they are allowed to take control of an activity at the highest level.

In many sports it is common for ex-players to become officials once their playing careers are over. This is often the case in first-class cricket, for example, where ex-players become umpires using a lot of the knowledge they gained as players.

Being an official can often be rather a thankless task as it is almost impossible to please everyone. There is increased pressure on modern officials because their decisions can be analysed on television replays. However, without these people being in charge it would be impossible for the events to take place.

The responsibilities of the officials can vary. Their main job is to take charge and control the activity. There are two main types of officials. **Senior officials** include:

- referees
- judges
- umpires.

Minor officials include:

- linesmen and women
- assistant referees
- timekeepers
- scorers.

All officials have to work together to make sure the sporting event runs smoothly. Other responsibilities they can have include:

- interpreting the rules, laws or regulations of the activity;
- checking the equipment to be used;
- making sure the correct number of players are taking part;
- timing the activity.

Fourth officials

At professional football matches there is always a reserve official, called the fourth official, who assists the referee. He or she can take the place of any of the match officials. If the referee is unable to carry on for some reason, then usually the most senior assistant referee will take his or her place and the fourth official would become an assistant referee. At the FIFA World Cup in 2006 there were five officials!

Skills

The skills that an official must have do not really differ between sports. They can be summarized as follows:

• *A full and thorough knowledge of the rules or regulations of the activity* – as the officials cannot usually refer to a rule book during a game, they must be prepared for, and know how to deal with, any incidents that might occur. Some sports have very complicated rules and some have so many it is almost impossible to know them all. In golf, for example, there are even local rules that apply only to a particular golf course. When sports have a complicated system such as this, the official in charge may need

Officials often need to consult on some decisions.

assistance and rulings can take some time to be finalized.

• *A fair approach to the game* – which means that the official does not favour one of the teams or players but is **impartial**. To make sure of this many activities at the highest level have **neutral** officials who may even come from a different country.

• *Being firm and decisive* – when they are in charge, officials may need to prevent any arguments starting. Their decision is usually final, so they must stick to it. Players respect firm and confident officials who communicate decisions clearly.

• *Good physical condition* – which may be as simple as having good eyesight and/or enough speed and basic fitness to keep up with the game they are controlling. Some sports require their officials to take an annual fitness test and some have a maximum age for officials, which is really a retirement age. This obviously only refers to sports where the referee has to play a physically active part.

Coaches

Coaches play a very important part in any sport. A coach is usually a specialist in one activity and is responsible for helping a competitor with:

• correcting and improving technique;

• acquiring new skills;

• improving their physical condition and maintaining it during the sporting season;

• supporting their mental preparation to get their best out of training and in competition.

Coaches usually work with performers at higher levels as it is a very demanding task. Many coaches work full-time and are paid. In many individual activities, such as international athletics, many of the top performers employ a personal coach who works with them, and even travels with them, most of the time. A coach can assist a performer or a team with:

- *preparing performances* – including choosing tactics, formations, strategies, game plans and fitness levels;

- *analysing performances* – by giving plenty of feedback, both during and after a performance, to help players to find ways to improve;

- *motivation and encouragement* – before or during a competition or performance, this can make the difference between a performer winning or losing;

- *reviewing performances* – by examining the last performance in great detail to look for ways in which improvements can be made, and to suggest any changes that might be needed.

One of the most important jobs of the coach is to analyse performances. This analysis can include the sportsperson's actions or even those of opponents. Each sport also has equipment that can aid coaching and training. For example, cricketers practise in cricket nets, trampolinists may use harnesses, rugby players use scrummage machines and tennis players can use an automatic ball feeder. A top-level coach must know how to use the most modern equipment effectively and safely.

Coaches can help to improve a performance.

Analysing a recording of a performance can be a valuable training aid.

There are some common aids that can be used by coaches in all activities:

- *Video* – TV and other video recordings are now one of the coach's most important aids. They can record other people's performances to show how something should be done. They can also record their own players to let them watch and analyse their own performance. Digital video can be replayed in slow motion, which can show every little detail, as the movements can be filmed from a variety of angles. For example, a trampolinist who is travelling (moving forwards in the air when rotating) can benefit a great deal from watching it replayed, because they can actually see how far they are travelling and correct it.

- *Demonstrations* – many coaches are ex-players or performers and they are therefore often able to demonstrate the right way to do something. If they cannot do this themselves, they can usually find someone else who can and they can then point out the good features being shown. Sometimes they will take their team or players to watch a team of a higher standard, for the same reasons.

- *Books and coaching manuals* – coaches can recommend suitable books for performers to study. It is also very important for them to be able to keep up-to-date themselves. They may have to read a lot of articles in journals and keep up with current developments and any changes in rules.

- *Other specialists* – to prepare their performers fully, coaches may enlist the help of people such as:

  - **dieticians** (to work out the correct diet for the particular event);

  - **sports psychologists** (this has become an important area as many coaches know that a performer's mental state can be a very significant factor in how well they do);

  - qualified **physiotherapists** (to deal with minor injuries, strains or pulls, and **rehabilitation**);

  - team doctors (to deal with emergencies).

- *Coaching boards* – these are display boards marked out with the playing area or pitch. The coach uses them during a game to point out positional changes or tactics.

- *Visual analysis programmes* – these are computer-linked programmes that record physical performance. They allow the participants to review what they have done or even compare it to another similar performance. They are now used widely to allow students to analyse and improve their own performances.

Many advances have been made in recent years that can help to monitor, assist and even predict performances. Developments in computer software and digital technology are among the most significant and many useful programs and devices are now available.

Specialist computer software can help select the most suitable training schedules for individual performers. Monitors carried by the performers can be linked directly into computers while training is taking place, to see what the effects are. For example, many competitors in long distance cycling events have specially fitted chest and wrist monitors. The monitors record information such as heart rate and feed the data to small monitors on a cyclist's handlebar. This gives cyclists an indication of just how hard their bodies are working and the limits to which they can push themselves.

Competitive situations can be **simulated** by computers so that a performer can virtually experience a game or competition and work out ways to play. Some Formula One racing drivers use very advanced computer games to simulate a race on a circuit that they have not driven before. This means they do not have to go to the circuit to become familiar with it.

More advanced equipment and training aids are being designed. These include the materials that are being used, such as lightweight clothing and lighter, safer equipment.

One of the most important aids for a coach is a very accurate timing device. Being able to record split times or lap times with a countdown facility is vital. These functions can be handled by wrist watches designed for particular sports.

Trainers

Trainers can perform a different role to coaches and play an important part in many sports. Their two main responsibilities are:

- *setting training schedules* – this can be over a long or short period of time and will be based on ensuring fitness levels and getting performers ready for competitions;

- *taking training sessions* – most clubs or individuals need someone to take on this most basic task. The trainer makes sure that all the right things are included in each session, such as a warm-up. The main aim is to achieve the correct fitness level for every performer.

Many cyclists wear monitors to check their heart rates.

For there to be high standards in any sport, there must be some rules that say exactly how the sport should be played. These rules are also called laws or regulations.

All sports have rules covering:

- basic organization
- ease of administration
- safety
- enjoyment.

Most of the rules for the sports people enjoy today have developed over a long period of time. In the distant past, sporting activities did not have many set rules. However, as sports became more popular, and more widely played, it became necessary to set out basic guidelines, for the reasons listed above.

Basics

The playing area or surface to be used has to be defined and clearly stated. It is often important to standardize the length of time of the activity, the clothing to be worn, the equipment used and the number of people to take part.

Safety

One of the most important reasons for the introduction of rules is safety. Many of our present-day activities would be very dangerous if there were not very strict rules about foul play and the equipment to be used. Many of the rule changes that are made are to make sports safer.

Who makes the rules?

There are official bodies that set the rules for all of the activities that take place in this country. There are also international organizations that set the rules for sport all over the world. In tennis, for example, the International Tennis Federation (ITF) has responsibility for the rules that apply throughout the world. The ITF can over-rule decisions made by the Lawn Tennis Association, which sets the rules for the UK.

Many activities also have players' associations, which work closely with the ruling bodies, setting and often – more importantly – enforcing the rules! These players' associations are more common in **professional** sport than they are in **amateur** sport.

Breaking the rules can be costly. Chelsea's Michael Ballack holds his head as he is sent off in a fottball match against Liverpool.

Etiquette

Not all of the rules of an activity are actually written down; some of them are just 'accepted' by the people who take part. This is often known as **etiquette** and often takes the form of fair play, good manners or good sporting attitude.

In all activities there is accepted etiquette that it is not in the 'rule book'. It is up to the participants to behave in the right way. There is no real way to ensure that this does happen but players are very unpopular if they do not conform. This is another reason why there are players' associations. They will often take action against someone who is in breach of etiquette. Here are some examples of good etiquette:

- *Football* – if an opponent is injured, a player will kick the ball out of play to stop the match and allow the injured player to have treatment. On the re-start throw-in, the team will throw the ball back to their opponents who originally kicked the ball out of play. Unfortunately, there has been some **controversy** about players feigning injury in order to stop opponents' attacking moves.

- *Tennis* – at the end of a match, opponents shake hands and also thank and shake hands with the umpire.

- *Squash* – players will call their own foul shots such as 'double hit' and 'ball not up'.

Changes to rules

Rule changes can come about:

- to make the activity safer;

- to make the activity more exciting in order to attract more players or spectators;

- to keep up with the developments or changes in equipment or materials used.

Enforcement of rules

Rule enforcement is important and there is a system in all sports to make sure that it takes place. If a player does not abide by the rules, penalties include:

- suspension

- a ban

- a fine

- expulsion from the sport.

All sports have penalties that can be applied when the game is in progress, such as the yellow and red card system in football, the **sin bin** in ice hockey, rugby league and rugby union, and the fouled-out system in basketball. For more serious offences, action will be taken after the event has ended. This can be for drug and doping violations, extreme foul play, illegal payments or 'bringing the game into disrepute' – doing something that may not be directly related to the sport or match, but which damages the 'image' of the sport. Increasingly, video evidence is being used to discipline players, especially if match officials have not acted at the time of an incident.

Trialling new rules

Many of the international bodies change or amend rules in competitions that they organize, so that they can try the new rules out. This gives the governing bodies a chance to see how successful the changes are before introducing them throughout the world.

Sport England

Sport England is the body responsible for promoting and investing in English sport. It helps the government meet its sporting objectives and distributes both **Lottery** and government funds to sport. Since 1994 Sport England has invested about £2 billion into sport in England.

It has three main objectives, identified as:

• *Start* – to improve the health of the nation, particularly for disadvantaged groups;

• *Stay* – continue this through a thriving network of clubs, coaches and volunteers, and a commitment to equity (fairness);

• *Succeed in sport* – working through an **infrastructure** capable of developing world class performers.

Sport England operates through nine regional offices and targets sports development through work with the following organizations and groups:

• Government

• Local authorities

• Health professionals

• National governing bodies

• Teachers

• The voluntary sector

• The commercial sector

Sport England is able to share best practice, set standards, and build partnerships with other organizations. It promotes the benefits of sport including healthier living, **social inclusion** and crime prevention. Through its website (www.sportengland.org) it provides information about activities, clubs, events and resources.

One of the most important roles that Sport England carries out is to be in overall charge of the five National Sports Centres, which are:

• *Bisham Abbey* – this is located in Buckinghamshire. It has recently benefited from a £10 million redevelopment and includes facilities such as a £1.2 million international hockey pitch, indoor tennis centre, dojo halls for Judo, community gym and squash courts, a nine-hole golf course, a sports therapy performance unit and accommodation for over 90 athletes

• *Crystal Palace* – this is located in London. It has an internationally renowned athletic stadium, a central grassed area, two synthetic floodlight pitches and extensive indoor facilities, including four

UK Sport encourages and supports all types of sport, including canoeing.

swimming pools. In addition there are an indoor athletics track, badminton courts, basketball courts and indoor cricket and hockey areas. Crystal Palace also houses one of the country's leading sports injury clinics, which has resident specialists in orthopaedics, rheumatology, cardiology, thoracic medicine, nutrition, physiotherapy and podiatry.

- *Holme Pierrepoint* – this is located near Nottingham and is the National Water Sports Centre. It is set in over 100 hectares of parkland with three distinct pieces of water that include a regatta lake, a purpose built canoe slalom course and a water ski lagoon. These facilities enable dinghy sailing, windsurfing, canoeing, rowing, water skiing and power boat handling to be offered. The River Trent is accessible from the centre. The indoor facilities include an indoor training hall and a sports science and medicine centre that offers sports injury **rehabilitation** and **physiological** testing.

- *Lilleshall* – this is located in Newport and has achieved British Olympic Association approval for the quality of its training facilities for gymnastics and archery. There are many indoor and outdoor facilities including tennis courts, a gymnastic training hall, two multi-purpose sports halls, a floodlight astroturf pitch, specialist archery and cricket halls and a six lane flat green bowls lawn. The centre is also home to the Lilleshall Human Performance Centre, which carries out physiological assessments, nutrition and physical activity training programmes and medical education for athletes and coaches.

- *Plas y Brenin* – this is located in Snowdon in North Wales and is the National Centre for the Mountains. It offers mountaineering, climbing and canoeing. Other facilities include a climbing and training wall, an indoor canoe training pool, an artificial ski slope and a fitness room.

Sports organizations often arrange training and coaching sessions for young people to help raise standards.

Not all sports have to be physically demanding!

UK Sport

This organization was established by Royal Charter in 1996. UK Sport works in partnership with the home country sports councils and other agencies to lead sport in the UK to world-class success. It is responsible for managing and distributing public money, which means it is the body responsible for distributing all of the funds for sport raised by the National Lottery. It is accountable to Parliament through the Department for Culture, Media & Sport.

UK Sport has a clear mission to work in partnership with other organizations. It also has clearly stated goals, which are in three particular categories.

- *World Class Performance* – 'World-class performance can only be delivered by world-class personnel and the challenge in the Beijing Olympiad is to develop home grown expertise to support our athletes.'

- *Worldwide Impact* – 'Our international programme will enable us to bring best practice in other sporting nations to the UK. We will also provide clear strategic support to enable sports to bid for and stage major events in this country.'

- *World Class Standards* – 'UK Sport will promote the highest standards of sporting conduct whilst continuing to lead a

world-class anti-doping programme for the UK and being responsible for improving the education and promotion of ethically fair and drug free sport.'

UK Sport has identified specific ways in which it is striving to achieve these goals.

Investing in sport

Since 1997 UK Sport has operated manyprogrammes designed to support leading Olympic and Paralympic athletes in their mission to win medals at the world's biggest sporting events. With only limited funding available, money has always been directed at those sports and individuals that can demonstrate that they have the capability to deliver medal-winning performances. This funding is targeted at the athletes via their sport's governing body. They are supported by a performance programme that includes coaching, training and competition support, medical and scientific services and access to the best facilities that the UK has to offer. Athletes can receive a contribution towards living and sporting costs through a means tested 'Athlete Personal Award'.

World Class Pathway

From 1 April 2006 UK Sport assumed full responsibility for all Olympic and Paralympic performance-related support in England, from the identification of talent to performing at the top level. It also provides expert high-performance consultancy to non-Olympic sports in England, to help improve performance and drive success in the future.

Scottish, Welsh and Northern Ireland athletes continue to be funded by their home countries until they reach world class performance levels, but they can then transfer to the pathway programme.

This pathway operates at three levels:

- *World Class Podium* – this supports athletes who have a realistic medal capability at the next Olympics, four years away from the event;

- *World Class Development* – this is the pathway immediately below the Podium level for athletes approximately six years away from the event;

- *World Class Talent* – this programme is designed to support the identification of athletes who have the potential to progress through the World Class Pathway even if they are currently eight years away from an event.

This programme is designed to ensure that the UK is fully prepared for the 2012 Olympic Games to be held in London and has been developed since the successful bid in 2005.

Sports Coach UK (The National Coaching Foundation)

This is a charitable organization dedicated to the development and implementation of coaches and coaching throughout the UK. It has twelve regional workshops throughout the UK, including Scotland, Northern Ireland and Wales. It has established a UK Action Plan for Coaching, which commenced in 2006, particularly focusing on preparation for the 2012 Olympics and beyond to the 2014 Commonwealth Games.

Water sports and recreation is one of the areas to have benefited from increased support from the UK's sports organizations.

The Central Council of Physical Recreation (CCPR)

The CCPR is the independent, voluntary umbrella organization for the national governing and representative bodies of sport and recreation in the UK. It promotes, protects and develops the interests of sport and physical recreation at all levels. It also provides support and services to those who participate in and administer sport and recreation, so is active in sport politics. It does not allocate any funds to governing bodies.

The membership of the CCPR is made up of the governing or representative bodies for each sports or recreational activity:

- About 270 national governing and representative bodies of sport and recreation;

- About 150,000 voluntary sports clubs;

- Millions of individuals who participate in sport and recreation.

The CCPR considers itself to be the voice of British sport. It aims to lobby and represent the views of members to all authorities whose decisions have an impact on sport and recreation. It provides its members with advice and information on issues relating to the running of their sport and business. It ensures all of its members are kept informed of changes in government policy and UK and EU (European Union) law.

The CCPR takes an active approach to influencing government policies, such as recommending legislative measures (laws and regulations) on issues affecting sport and recreation. It also co-ordinates its members' views on legislation as it passes through the UK and national parliaments. As well as working with bodies in the UK, the CCPR has close links with its European counterparts. This happens through ENGSO (European Non-Governmental Sports Organizations), which represents the views of sports bodies throughout Europe.

Further details regarding the role of the CCPR can be found on its website www.ccpr.org.uk.

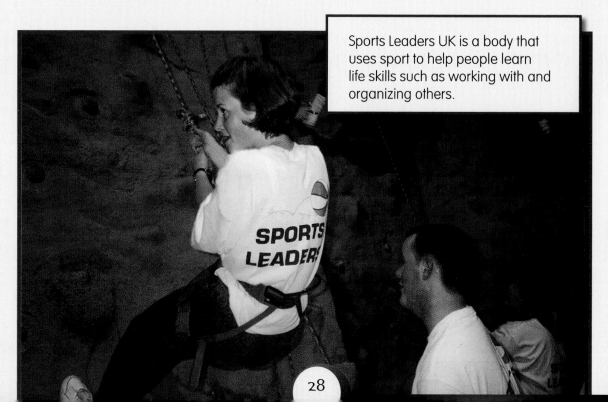

Sports Leaders UK is a body that uses sport to help people learn life skills such as working with and organizing others.

Governing bodies

Each sport has to be separately organized and administered. The main responsibilities of the governing bodies that do this are:

- arranging local and national competitions;

- selecting teams for international competitions such as the Olympic Games and the various world championships;

- keeping players and participants in their particular sport informed;

- maintaining relationships with the media;

- drafting the rules and laws of the game (and making any changes and amendments);

- advancing the special interest of their sport.

The National Trust

The National Trust was first formed in 1895 and it was given legal status in 1907 after the National Trust Act. This gave the Trust the right to designate its land 'inalienable'. This means that property and land that it owns cannot be sold or mortgaged; it will always be the property of the National Trust.

The Trust is a charity and it is the largest landowner and conservation society in the UK. Access to the land and property of the Trust is available to members, who pay an annual fee. However, much of the open land, moorland and coastal stretches are looked after and maintained by the Trust, and is freely accessible to everyone. Throughout the country it owns more than 260,000 hectares of open access land, with about a quarter of this in the Lake District. Many walkers and people who enjoy the pleasures of outdoor

activities are very grateful for the work the National Trust does, because it maintains all of these areas and keeps them available for their leisure pursuits.

The Trust operates in England, Wales and Northern Ireland; there is a separate National Trust for Scotland.

Governing bodies help to raise standards of coaching, and ensure it is available to talented performers.

National Trust skills

Volunteers bring many skills to the National Trust, from pilots and surveyors to gamekeepers and calligraphers (artists who specialize in handwriting).

Walkers in the Lake District making full use of the countryside.

Nature England

Nature England was formed by bringing together English Nature, the landscape access and recreation elements of the Countryside Agency, and the environmental land management functions of the Rural Development Service.

Nature England is aiming to work for people, places and nature, in order to enhance **biodiversity**, landscapes and wildlife in rural, urban, coastal and marine areas. It promotes access to natural England, recreation and public well-being, and contributes to the way natural resources are managed.

The organization has four strategic aims:

• A healthy natural environment, by conserving and enhancing England's natural places;

• Sustainable use and management of the natural environment

• Enjoyment of the natural environment, with more people enjoying, understanding and acting to improve the natural environment

• Decisions that collectively secure the future of the natural environment.

The Arts Council

The Arts Council was established in 1946. In 1994 it was replaced by three new bodies: the Arts Council of England, the Arts Council of Scotland and the Arts Council of Wales. There is also an Arts Council for Northern Ireland. These are the main funding bodies for the arts in their respective areas and are therefore very important to certain areas of sporting activity, such as dance.

The councils have a responsibility for developing and improving the knowledge and understanding of the arts. They are also responsible for increasing the accessibility of the arts to the general public. Their particular responsibility for dance is one of the most important areas in which they work. There is a requirement that dance is taught in schools so organizational links with the Arts Council have become vital.

The Arts Councils receive money from central government. They have also benefited

Volunteers

Over 50 million hours are given by volunteers every year to help organize sporting and recreational activities in the UK, at all levels.

greatly from funds from the National Lottery, which have enabled them to carry out their responsibilities more widely. Dance is just one area of the performing arts where they assist, and even individuals are able to benefit from some help with funding.

Youth organizations

Many youth organizations provide sporting and leisure activities especially for young people. They mainly fall into two categories:

- youth clubs and organizations;

- uniformed organizations such as the Guides Association, the Scout Association and the Air Training Corps.

These groups often promote outdoor pursuits, providing training and expertise. Many of them run their own award schemes, which

provide a very good basic knowledge. They also have access to (or own) facilities that are used for various leisure activities, and frequently run competitions.

International Olympic Committee (IOC)

This is the governing body of the Olympic Games. Its main functions include:

- selecting **host cities** for the summer and winter games;

- approving the sports to be included in the Olympics;

- working with the host city, international governing bodies and international sports federations to plan the games.

Dance performances can be staged in water.

Members of the IOC used to be elected by existing members, but now places are made available for athletes, members of governing bodies, and National Olympic Committee leaders. These representatives may be elected from any nation that has a national Olympic committee.

Members used to be elected for life, but must now retire at the age of 70. They elect an executive board which handles many decisions; this is led by a president, four vice-presidents and ten other members.

Membership of the IOC brings with it a lot of responsibility. Places are highly sought-after, because the committee has such an influence on where the games are to be held, and how the Olympic movement promotes and supports sport around the world. Bidding to host the games is a complicated and expensive business that involves governments as well as the bidding cities. The IOC committee members are required to assess all aspects of the bids from the cities that would like to stage the games. There has often been **controversy** over their choice.

The Paralympic Games are organized by the International Paralympic Committee. This is the international organization of elite sports for athletes with disabilities.

Londoners in Trafalgar Square celebrate London's selection in July 2005 as the city that will host the 2012 Olympic Games. London beat Paris and three other cities to win the summer games.

British Olympic Association (BOA)

The BOA works closely with the IOC. It provides the foundation for Team GB to work around before and during Olympic Games.

Working with the Olympic governing bodies, the BOA selects Team GB from the best sportswomen and men. They will compete in the 28 summer and 7 winter Olympic sports. The BOA is not funded by government and has no political interest, so it is completely dependent upon commercial sponsorship and fund-raising income. It works very closely with athletes and their national governing bodies, assisting them in their preparations for, and performance at, Olympic Games.

The BOA is the strong, independent voice of British Olympic sport. Its role is to lead and prepare the nation's finest athletes at the Olympic Games and it also has the responsibility for developing the Olympic movement throughout the UK.

The BOA gives athletes access to world-class preparation camps, as well as providing management, coaching and athlete training so that every competitor feels well prepared to deal with the unique environment of an Olympic Games.

Leading up to a Games, the BOA organizes visits to the host city, giving team leaders from each sport the opportunity to fine-tune their preparations before competitors arrive for Olympic competition.

Currently the BOA is concentrating its efforts on responding to the decision made on Wednesday 6 July 2005 when the IOC awarded the 2012 Games to London. An organization known as LOCOG (London Organizing Committee for the Olympic Games) has been formed to assemble the required land, obtain all the necessary planning permission and arrange funding. The Government is responsible for the appropriate legislation, security, immigration, the delivery of its guarantees and the overall underwriting of the cost of the 2012 Games.

The BOA has three core commitments to the 2012 Olympic Project, which are:

• To secure UK Olympic and Paralympic success at the Games;

• To promote, through sport, the Olympic ideals across the 2012 programme;

• To set up a London Olympic institute to support elite athletes and encourage participation in sport.

The BOA has also committed itself to ensure that sport remains high on the political agenda and plays a full role in the social life of the UK's citizens. It wants to fulfil the London bid's promise to leave behind a real **legacy** for future generations of sportspeople.

BOA fund-raising

The BOA appears to become more active in the period just before an Olympic Games, as it tries to raise the money needed to send the British team to the games. In fact it works non-stop to raise the funds but lifts its profile even more as the Games approach.

International sport

The Olympic Games

The earliest recorded Olympic Games took place in 776 BC in the stadium of Olympia, in ancient Greece, from where the Olympics get their name. They were held in honour of the God Zeus. The stadium in which the games took place was quite impressive, as there was enough room for 40,000 spectators.

The Games were held every four years. All hostilities between the warring Greek states were stopped while the Games took place. Typical events at that time were wrestling, boxing, running (the main event was over 200 metres), discus, javelin, long jump and chariot racing. It is interesting to note that nearly all of those events still take place today.

The Games carried on in this way for many years until the reign of Emperor Theodosius in AD 394. He stopped them because he believed that the Games had lost their religious meaning and that the performers only took part for the riches of winning. It would be interesting to find out what the emperor would think of the Olympics as they exist today!

The Olympics were not held again for hundreds of years. Then, in 1896, they were re-launched in Athens, Greece. The links with the original Olympics went further than simply holding them in the same country. Many traditions were established, based on the old Games. Before the start of each Olympic Games, a torch is lit at Olympia using the Sun's rays. This torch is carried by a relay of runners to the next **host city's** stadium, and used to light a flame, which then burns throughout the Games.

The remains of the Colosseum in Rome show how large the stadiums were for ancient sporting events. They could hold as many spectators as most modern stadiums.

The modern Olympics

The Olympic Games that have taken place since 1896 are referred to as the modern Olympics. They were re-started mainly through the efforts and determination of one man. Baron Pierre de Coubertin was a French educationalist who had been very impressed by the way that sport was organized in England. This, together with the fact that in 1875 some German archaeologists had discovered the ruins of the original stadium in Olympia, made him decide to start up a movement to re-introduce the Games. In 1894 the International Olympic Committee was formed and it set about the task of organizing the games for 1896.

Baron de Coubertin believed that the Olympic movement that he had founded would promote world peace and harmony. One of his famous quotes is displayed on the scoreboard at the opening of each games, as it is what he based his ideas on. It is also often kept on display during the Games:

"The most important thing in the Olympic Games is not to win but to take part. Just as the most important thing in life is not the triumph but the struggle."

The **International Olympic Committee (IOC)** originally consisted of people chosen by de Coubertin himself, but it is now a very large body with representatives from all of the participating nations. This committee decides where the games are to be held.

It was de Coubertin who decided that the Games should move all around the world and be awarded to a city rather than to a country. Now, cities have to make a bid to stage the Olympic Games and the final decision is made over six years in advance, to give the host city enough time to prepare

and get all of the facilities ready. At one time, not many cities were prepared to host the Games because they were very expensive and usually ran at a loss.

This situation changed after the 1984 Olympic Games in Los Angeles, USA, where the marketing and sponsorship of the Games resulted in a surplus being made. In theory, the Games should not run at a profit, which is why they used the word 'surplus'. Once cities – and countries – realized that there was an opportunity to promote themselves, improve facilities and standards and make money as well, the whole business of bidding for and staging the Games took on more importance. Now, a huge effort is made just to bid to be the host city.

Paralympic games

In 1948 Dr Ludwig Guttman was director of the National Spinal Injuries Centre at Stoke Mandeville Hospital. He organized competitive sports for people with spinal injuries at the Stoke Mandeville Games. Soon people with other disabilities and from other nations became involved.

Olympic Games facts

• At the first modern Olympics of 1896, thirteen nations entered and the total number of athletes was 285. All of these were men because no women were allowed to enter!

• The Olympic closing ceremony finishes with the releasing of doves to symbolize the peaceful spirit of the Games.

In 1960, a four-yearly 'parallel Olympics' began. In that year over 400 athletes from 23 countries competed in Rome. This had grown to 3,806 athletes from 136 countries competing in 19 sports in the 2004 Paralympics in Athens.

The Paralympic Games have always been held in the same year as the Olympic Games. Since the 1988 Seoul summer games and the 1992 Albertville winter games, they have also taken place at the same venues as the Olympic Games.

The table below shows where the various summer and winter Olympic Games have taken place since they were re-introduced in 1896.

Year	Summer	Winter
1896	Athens, Greece	Not held
1900	Paris, France	Not held
1904	St Louis, USA	Not held
1908	London, England	Not held
1912	Stockholm, Sweden	Not held
1916	World War I – no games held	
1920	Antwerp, Belgium	Not held
1924	Paris, France	Chamonix, France
1928	Amsterdam, Holland	St Moritz, Switzerland
1932	Los Angeles, USA	Lake Placid, USA
1936	Berlin, Germany	Garmisch, Germany
1940	World War II – no games held	
1944	World War II – no games held	
1948	London, England	St Moritz, Switzerland
1952	Helsinki, Finland	Oslo, Norway
1956	Melbourne, Australia	Cortina, Italy
1960	Rome, Italy	Squaw Valley, USA
1964	Tokyo, Japan	Innsbruck, Austria
1968	Mexico City	Grenoble, France
1972	Munich, Germany	Sapporo, Japan
1976	Montréal, Canada	Innsbruck, Austria
1980	Moscow, USSR	Lake Placid, USA
1984	Los Angeles, USA	Sarajevo, Yugoslavia
1988	Seoul, S. Korea	Calgary, Canada
1992	Barcelona, Spain	Albertville, France
1994		Lillehammer, Norway
1996	Atlanta, USA	Nagano, Japan
2000	Sydney, Australia	
2002		Salt Lake City, USA
2004	Athens, Greece	
2006		Torino, Italy
2008	Beijing, China	
2010		Vancouver, Canada
2012	London, England	

From 2008 on, the Paralympics will always take place just after the Olympic Games, using the same sporting venues and facilities. The Paralympics are now elite sport events for athletes from six different disability groups. They emphasize the participants' athletic achievements rather than their disability and competition is as fierce as the Olympics themselves.

Individual Games

The Olympic Games were the first major international sporting event. They are still the most important and successful of all of the events that take place. However, things have not always run smoothly and nearly all of the recent Games have been affected by problems of one sort or another. The following is a brief description of the major events which have affected recent games.

Berlin, 1936

The decision to award these Games to Berlin was made in 1931, two years before Adolph Hitler and his Nazi party came to power in Germany.

One of Hitler's main beliefs was that there was a master race, known as the Aryans. Supposedly, these people were blond and fair-skinned and were true Germans. The Nazis despised the Jews. By the time of the Olympic Games the Nazis had started to persecute the Jews and introduce separate laws for them.

Hitler tried to use the Games to promote all these ideas, turning the games into a propaganda exercise. One of the main reasons he failed was the success of a black American athlete, Jesse Owens.

Jesse Owens won four gold medals in the track and field events, much to Hitler's obvious disapproval. The US team had only narrowly voted to attend the Games because of Hitler's well-known views on black athletes and Jews. The success of the many black athletes in the US team was an embarrassment for Hitler and stopped him achieving what he had set out to do in terms of propaganda.

Jesse Owens competing in Berlin in 1936.

Games apart

The Games organizers decided that from 1994 the winter and summer Olympics should be staged two years apart, so some of the winter competitors would be able to take part in two Games in two years. This had never happened before.

Mexico City, 1968

The main **controversy** about these Games was that they had been awarded to Mexico City in the first place! This was because the city is situated at very high altitude, which helps the performance of athletes who usually train in these conditions. It also assists athletes in the shorter, more explosive events. There was genuine concern for performers in longer events, in case the **rarefied** atmosphere caused breathing difficulties.

The cost of staging the event was also criticized. Mexico was a very poor country and a vast amount of money was spent on staging the Games. The city of Tokyo, which had staged the Games four years earlier, had spent about £100 million (then a huge sum) and it was doubtful if Mexico could really afford the money to pay for the Games.

The Games were also overshadowed by the death of many Mexican students, shot by security forces during a politcal protest just ten days before the event.

During a medal ceremony, some black American athletes gave a 'Black Power' salute, by each raising a black-gloved fist. The first and third runners in the 200 metres, Tommie Smith and John Carlos, as well as the 440-metre relay team, were sent home for doing this. The athletes took this action to highlight the way that black people were treated in the United States. There was still a great deal of prejudice against black citizens in the United States at the time. The athletes chose this way to make their protest and make the world more aware of the problem.

One of the Palestinian terrorists with a member of the negotiating team during the hostage crisis in 1972.

Munich, 1972

There was another Black Power protest by two Americans, Vince Matthews and Wayne Collett, during a medal ceremony when they failed to stand to attention. However, these Games were completely dominated by a terrorist attack on some of the athletes.

There was unrest in the Middle East and a group of Palestinian terrorists attacked members of the Israeli team. Eight terrorists attacked the Israeli quarters in the **Olympic village**. They killed two of the team and took nine others hostage. After a gun battle (seen throughout the world on television), all of the hostages, five terrorists and a German police officer were killed.

The security aspects of staging the Games were highlighted and were to become a major consideration for all future Games.

Montréal, 1976

South Africa had been banned from the Games since 1964 (Tokyo), because of the apartheid policy that existed in the country. However, a rugby team from New Zealand had toured South Africa and so had upset most of the other African nations. The African nations threatened to boycott the Games unless the New Zealand team was banned.

New Zealand did take part and so the African nations stayed away. Altogether a total of 30 nations did not go. This was to be the start of a long period of boycotts for various reasons.

The financial cost of these Games was also very high. Because of the incident in Munich the security had to be greatly increased. This was on top of the enormous cost of staging the Games. The city of Montréal continued to pay off the debt of staging the Games for many years.

Moscow, 1980

The choice of Moscow for these Games had been controversial because the Soviet Union had a poor record on human rights. However, it was one of the most successful competing countries in the history of the Olympics and had never hosted the Games before.

In 1979 the Soviet Union invaded the neighbouring country of Afghanistan. It still had an invasion force there in 1980 at the start of the Games. It was too late to change the venue for the Games but many countries demanded that the Soviet Union withdraw its forces or they would boycott the Games. The Soviet Union refused to do this and many countries had to decide whether or not to send their competitors. Some countries, such as the United States, refused to send any. Great Britain advised its competitors not to go, but did not stop them if they wanted to. Many individuals also decided not to go.

Many thought that the Games were devalued because of this. The standard was lower with so many strong teams (such as the Americans) absent from the Games. However, more world records were set than in the Games in Montréal.

Flying the flag

At the Moscow Games, fifteen nations (Australia, Andorra, Belgium, Denmark, France, Great Britain, Ireland, Italy, Luxembourg, the Netherlands, Portugal, Puerto Rico, San Marino, Spain and Switzerland) marched under the Olympic flag instead of their national flags.

Part of the Olympic Games' lavish opening ceremony.

Los Angeles, 1984

As the venue was chosen six years in advance, the International Olympic Committee could not avoid a US city staging the Games immediately after the United States had boycotted those at Moscow in the Soviet Union. The two countries did not have good relations and there was a great fear that the Soviet Union would boycott the games as a way of retaliating against the United States. This is exactly what happened!

The Soviet Union and fifteen other nations, boycotted the Games. The official reason most gave was concern over security arrangements. There was still ill-feeling between the United States and the Soviet Union over the invasion of Afghanistan and there were threats of demonstrations in United States against the Soviet competitors.

There is little doubt that the worry about security was a convenient excuse for the Soviet Union to get its own back. Nearly all the other countries that boycotted were influenced by the Soviet Union, as they were also **communist**-ruled countries. The Soviet Union organized a set of 'Friendship Games' as an alternative event.

Another excuse was that the Games were being over-commercialized. The staging of the Games and its organization followed the American tradition of showmanship and the opening ceremony was one of the most spectacular ever seen. It set a precedent for other host cities to come up with similar very lavish ceremonies in future years. The whole event was sponsored by large, international companies and, for the first time, the Games ran at a large profit. This use of large-scale sponsorship was something that had come to stay and was used at later Games. However, all of this went against communist beliefs.

Seoul, 1988

Seoul is in South Korea, which had a long-standing dispute with the neighbouring country of North Korea. There had been a war between the two countries in 1952 and the situation in 1988 was not much better. The IOC was greatly criticized for awarding Seoul the Games. There was much concern, right up until the start, that the facilities would not be ready and that the North Koreans would interfere. The North Koreans had already demanded that they be allowed to stage some of the events.

Competing nations

In terms of the number of countries competing, Seoul was the most successful Games up until that time – 1988 – with 160 nations competing (compared to the 13 nations who took part in 1896).

In the end there was very little disruption and the Games were quite successful. There was another boycott by five countries, including North Korea and Cuba. It is likely that more countries would have considered boycotting. However, the IOC had introduced a rule that if countries did boycott the Games, all their officials would be excluded and not allowed to take part in decision-making. This clearly deterred many from a boycott.

The main controversy at these games involved positive drugs tests. Altogether, ten athletes were banned after testing positive for taking **performance-enhancing drugs**. The most famous was the Canadian sprinter, Ben Johnson. He had won the 100 metres in a world record time but was then stripped of his title two days later.

Barcelona, 1992

After all the controversial events that had gone before, the 1992 Games were just about incident-free.

There was still some drug controversy as three British competitors – sprinter Jason Livingstone, and weightlifters Andrew Saxton and Andrew Davies – tested positive and were sent home.

A great deal of political change had occurred since the 1988 Games. The Eastern European communist governments had collapsed and the Soviet Union had ceased to exist. This meant that there was no longer an East and a West German team but a single, unified German team. Also, all of the countries that had previously made up the Soviet Union now existed in their own right and were able to compete individually. There were twelve new competing countries from the former Soviet bloc and some individuals, who could not be considered to be from an affiliated nation, competed under the Olympic flag.

Another 'new' entry was South Africa, which was allowed to return to the Olympics for the first time since 1964. The South Africans had abolished the apartheid system. They entered a mixed-race team.

Numbers of sports

In Barcelona, the total number of sports was increased to 28, with the addition of badminton and baseball. The total number of medal events was increased by 20 to 257. There were over 12,000 athletes and officials involved in the Games, from 169 nations.

Weightlifter Andrew Davies, sent home from Barcelona for failing a drugs test.

Atlanta, 1996

The Games returned to the United States only twelve years after they had last been held there. This was slightly controversial in itself. The Games seemed to be going very smoothly, without any major incident except for some minor drug exclusions. However, there was a bomb explosion in one of the parks near to the Olympic athletic stadium, where there was entertainment for all the visitors and local people. Although the Games were not directly affected, the incident raised the whole issue of security again. It also affected the atmosphere and media coverage surrounding the events.

Another controversy involved the very high temperatures and humidity at that time of year in Atlanta. Special timings allowed some events to take place in the early hours of the morning. In all the equestrian events there were specially-constructed fans that sprayed water on to the riders and horses to prevent them from overheating.

All the barriers that had separated **amateur** and **professional** sport were broken down by this time. Many professional performers took part in their events in the Games. The most famous of these were the US basketball team and many of the leading tennis players from throughout the world.

The World Athletics Championships is organized by the IAAF, the International Association of Athletics Federations. Here David Weir of Great Britain celebrates as he wins gold in the men's 200 metres wheelchair race at the 2005 championships in Helsinki, Finland.

Sydney, 2000

The Sydney Games almost set records for cost as the main stadium cost more than £250 million. Its capacity of 110,000 included enough room to fit four Boeing 747 airliners side by side under the main arches. This was the first time Australia had hosted the Games since Melbourne in 1956. There were about 10,000 athletes from 199 nations at the Games. The United States were again the most successful nation with 40 gold medals.

These Games will be remembered not for problems, but for the achievement of two athletes in particular. Great Britain's Steve Redgrave won his fifth consecutive rowing gold medal and the Australian runner, Cathy Freeman, won the women's 400 metres. Freeman was of Aboriginal background and was an inspiring symbol of national **reconciliation** between **indigenous** and non-indigenous Australians.

Athens, 2004

After 108 years, Athens was chosen to host the event again in 2004. There were many concerns about the facilities being ready on time and there were also doubts about security, but the Games passed off smoothly.

Two of the leading Greek sprinters missed drugs tests before the Games and so could not compete. There was a steady stream of failed drugs tests during the two-week event, which resulted in three Olympic champions being stripped of their titles. It was claimed that the testing for these Games was the most thorough ever, which was why there were so many failed tests.

On the final day of the Games, an intruder pushed the leader of the men's marathon, Brazilian runner Vanderlei de Lima, into the crowd. De Lima eventually finished third and was awarded his bronze medal and an award for sportsmanship during the Games' closing ceremony.

But the Games were generally free of problems. US swimmer Michael Phelps won six gold medals and eight medals in total, an amazing feat. China showed itself to be an emerging sporting powerhouse by finishing second in the overall medal table.

Other international events

Commonwealth Games

The idea for staging some games for all the members of what had been the British Empire was first suggested in 1891. It was not until 1930 that the first such games took place. The venue was Hamilton in Ontario, Canada. At this time they were known as the British Empire Games. They have only been known as the Commonwealth Games since 1970.

The Games follow the format of the Olympics very closely. They are also held every four years, following the Olympics by two years. They have a reputation for being the 'friendly games' and have not been as disrupted by boycotts or scandals as the Olympics.

Athens facts

In Athens in 2004, over 11,000 athletes from 201 countries competed in 28 sports. The total number of medal events was increased to 301. There were over 5,500 team **officials** involved in the Games. Another 4,000 athletes took part in the Paralympics that followed.

Wimbledon

The original name of the Wimbledon tennis tournament was the 'All England Tennis Championships', but it has been open to players from any country. The Championship is widely regarded as one of the most important tennis tournaments, alongside the US, French and Australian Opens, and the Tennis Masters Cup.

Originally Wimbledon was the home of the All England Croquet Club. The members decided to use the very well-prepared and tended lawns for tennis, as well. The first championships were held in 1877 and, apart from breaks for the World Wars, they have been held every year since.

In 1968 the organizers took the very bold step of declaring the championship to be an **open event** so that amateurs and professionals could play. This was the first major international competition to take this step and it paved the way for the breakdown of these barriers in other sports.

World championships

Many sports now stage their own world championships, and these are becoming established as major international sporting events. Some of them have begun only recently but it is unusual to find any major sport that does not have one.

Wimbledon income

The large scale of the Wimbledon tournament can be seen by the money it generates. In 1998 it made a record £33 million profit. In 2005 it made about £27 million.

The Ryder Cup is contested every two years between teams of golfers from Europe and the United States. Irishman Darren Clarke celebrates after making a long putt during the final day of the competition in 2006.

Football

The world championship in football is usually known simply as the World Cup. This is because it was one of the very first world championships to be held in any of the major sports. The first World Cup took place in Uruguay in 1930. It had taken the ruling body of international football (FIFA) a long time to get it all organized. When the six member countries met in 1904 they decided to hold a tournament. The principle of the cup was not agreed until 1920, when the president of FIFA, Jules Rimet (after whom the first World Cup trophy was named), was influential in getting it underway. It remains one of the world's most popular televized international events.

Cricket

Cricket was quite late in organizing a world championship. This was mainly due to the nature of the game. At test level, a game lasts for five days and a tournament on this basis would be just about impossible to arrange. The development of one-day knockout games meant that cricket could be played in a format that could be used in a tournament.

The women's game staged the first World Cup in 1973. The first cricket World Cup for men didn't take place until 1975. It was played in England between the six test match playing nations plus Sri Lanka and East Africa. It is now held every four years, most recently in the Caribbean in 2007.

Rugby

The first Rugby World Cup occurred in 1987. It was based in New Zealand and Australia. New Zealand beat France in the final. The third tournament was held in South Africa. This was South Africa's first chance to host a major championship since the country had been re-admitted to world sport, and it

celebrated by winning. England successfully won this competition in 2003, beating Australia 20-17, and became the first northern hemisphere side to win the world title. Each of the tournaments held has been bigger and more successful than the last.

Athletics

The first athletics world championships were held in 1983 in Helsinki. They alternate with the indoor championships, which were first held in Paris in 1985. Both championships are held every two years.

There are many athletics championships held throughout the world today. There are separate ones for Africa, the Americas, the Caribbean, South-East Asia and the Arab States. There is even a World Student Games!

Specific matches and events

Some sports become international events because of the interest shown in a particular contest. This is often true with boxing, especially many of the world title contests, which can attract huge international television audiences for the various versions of the world titles that are available.

Test match series, such as those played in cricket and rugby, are also major events. Cricket tests between England and Australia, and between India and Pakistan, attract interest from many people who do not normally follow sport.

The **Superbowl** is the climax of the American Football season when the final game is played between the winners of the two conferences (that is, the two separate US leagues). It is the most-watched single television event ever broadcast!

Glossary

amateur someone who plays sport without being paid

apartheid political system that was in force in South Africa. Apartheid discriminated against people because of their race or colour.

biodiversity wide range of plants and animals in their natural environments

boycott refusing to attend an event as a protest

chairperson person in overall charge of a club

chief executive person in overall charge of a commercial company or professional organization

committee member person elected by the members of a club to run the club on their behalf

communism social system where economic wealth is shared amongst the whole community

competition format way in which a sports competition is organized

Conference football league that is the next highest to the Football League

constitution basic rules of how a club is run, which are accepted by all the members

controversial something that causes arguments and disagreements

de-motivates leads someone not to try so hard when competing

dieticians people who advise performers on their diet

dual provision where a school and a local community both use facilities at the same time

dual use where facilities are provided for school and community use at different times

etiquette unwritten law or regulation in a sport, which is usually followed by the players or performers

extra-curricular activities any activities that take place in a school outside set lesson times

governing body organization that runs and controls each particular sport

head-to-head final match played between the very best teams

host city city chosen to be the venue for an Olympic Games

impartial official who does not favour any one team or competitor over another

indigenous originally living in a place

infrastructure basic structure. In sport this means having facilities, clubs, coaches and competitions.

International Olympic Committee (IOC) the committee that, amongst other things, decides where the Games will be held

legacy something passed onto other people

line judge person who checks that the ball stays within the allowed areas in a game such as tennis

local authority the local, or nearest government for a certain area

match-up pairing up of different teams or players to take part in a competition against each other

media television, radio and the press

member someone who belongs to a club

media television, radio or the press

minor official someone who is qualified to take responsibility for the less senior aspects of a sporting event

National Lottery weekly prize draw that raises money for good causes, which include sport

net cord judge person responsible for checking that the net is kept at the right height, and that the ball passes clear of the net in a game such as tennis

neutral official who does not come from either team or the same country or area as either team

officials people who organize or run sporting events

Olympic village houses or flats that are specially built for the athletes to live in at the Olympic Games. Afterwards they may be used by the people living in the host country.

open days days on which there is free access to clubs for non-members

open event competition that can be entered by both amateur and professional performers

outdoor pursuits outdoor and adventurous activities

performance-enhancing drugs drugs that help someone perform better than they would if they did not take the drugs. Their use is against the rules.

physiological involved with how living things, such as our bodies, work

physiotherapists experts who help to treat sporting injuries

plate competition separate competition for first-round losers

play-off tie-breaker where two well-matched players or teams hold a short competition to see who will be the winner

professional someone who is paid for doing a job or for playing sport

promoted put up to a higher division

qualified trained to act as an official at an event

ranking position position in a special list that is made up by comparing how players of a particular sport perform

rarefied as applied to the atmosphere, thin and lacking in oxygen

reconciliation restoring friendly relations

rehabilitation recovery from injury or illness

relegated put down to a lower division

scouts staff from professional sports clubs who find and sign young players or performers

season times of year when a particular sport is played

secretary person who does the paperwork, letters and prepares the minutes for a committee

semi-professional sports player who gets paid for playing sport but who also works full- or part-time in another profession

senior official someone who has been trained or is experienced at the highest level, who runs or judges a sports event

simulation sporting situation that can be set up on a computer program

sin bin place where players must 'cool down' when temporarily sent off from the playing area

social inclusion including people from all groups in society

sports psychologists experts who help to prepare sports performers mentally

subscription money paid every year for membership of a club

Superbowl final match of the American football season that decides the overall champion

surplus amount of money left over when all the bills have been paid

taster sessions free sessions to try out activities at clubs

treasurer person who deals with the finances of a club

umpire person who oversees a match or game and makes sure that all the rules are followed

vice-chairperson person who looks after things when the chairperson is absent

Wolfendon Gap loss of interest in sport after leaving school. This pattern of behaviour is named after the writer of a report that looked at why young people gave up sport after they left school.

World Cup usually, the world championship competition for football, held every four years

Find out more

Books

Making of a Champion: A World-Class Sprinter, Clive Gifford (Heinemann Library, 2005)
Modern Olympic Games, Haydn Middleton (Heinemann Library, 2007)
Olympics, Chris Oxlade, David Ballheimer (DK Publishing, 2005)

Websites

British Olympic Association www.olympics.org.uk
Football Association www.thefa.com
Sport England www.sportengland.org

Sports Coach www.sportscoachuk.org
UK Sport www.uksport.gov.uk

Index